CRAFTING
WITH
WOODEN
CRATES & PALLETS

25 Simple Projects to Style Your Home

NATALIE WRIGHT

Dover Publications, Inc.
Mineola, New York

To my mother, Susan, and my father, Phillip,
whose passion for creating was intoxicating
to me as a child. Thank you for teaching me
all about making it myself to save money,
not being afraid to work with my hands,
and my favorite skill:
making awesome stuff with power tools.

Bibliographical Note
Crafting with Wooden Crates and Pallets is a new work,
first published by Dover Publications, Inc. in 2018.

International Standard Book Numbers
ISBN-13: 978-0-486-82423-9
ISBN-10: 0-486-82423-3

Manufactured in the United States by LSC Communications
82423301   2018
www.doverpublications.com

CONTENTS

INTRODUCTION

More and more stores are stocking their shelves with wooden crates, and it's no surprise that folks love them. Besides being inexpensive, crates offer a versatile way to style and decorate your home. From storage solutions to do-it-yourself (DIY) furniture, wooden crates are a resourceful way to organize your life on a budget. But where did this crazy crate trend come from?

Farmers first started using wooden crates for fruits and vegetables in the nineteenth century. Preprinted labels were glued on the ends of wooden crates to identify the contents, place of origin, and the packer's name. In the late 1950s, labels were no longer used because preprinted boxes replaced wooden crates, though they were still in high demand. Many farmers have turned to plastic and cardboard containers to ship their harvest, but you can find some farms that love the nostalgic smell and look of wood. Whether your produce comes in wooden or plastic containers, many of those vintage and antique crates still remain and are used in home decor and organization.

Today, crates are designed and made with the same inexpensive wood from days gone by. They come in a variety of shapes and sizes and can be found in just about every craft, home decor, and home improvement store. In *Crafting with Wooden Crates and Pallets*, I will show you twenty-five projects using crates and reclaimed pallet wood. Whether or not you are new to working with wood, there is something for everyone! Join me in decorating and organizing your home with these fun and versatile crafts.

UNDERSTANDING YOUR MATERIALS

SANDPAPER

For heavy sanding and stripping, you need coarse sandpaper measuring 40 to 60 grit. For smoothing surfaces and removing small imperfections, choose 80 to 120 grit sandpaper. For finishing surfaces, use superfine sandpaper with 360 to 600 grit.

BALSA WOOD

Balsa wood is the "miracle material" of the hobby world. It has the best strength-to-weight ratio of any other readily available material. Not only is it known for its high strength and low density, it can be easily shaped, sanded, glued, and painted despite its softness. Balsa is technically classified as a hardwood, rather than a softwood, because it has broad leaves and is not a conifer. Balsa wood can be found at both craft and home improvement stores and is fairly inexpensive to buy. It traditionally comes in sizes up to three feet and is easy to cut and sand.

WHITEWOOD BOARD

Whitewood board is typically a pinewood that is readily available and sold in a variety of sizes. Not only is it inexpensive, it is relatively easy to work with. You'll often find boards labeled "whitewood" that may be pine, spruce, fir, hemlock, or another similar species. You'll also see studs and construction lumber labeled "SPF," which means they could be made from pine, spruce, or fir trees. With the projects in this book, I primarily use inexpensive pine.

BASIC TOOLS

You will need a variety of tools that you may already have at home. If you don't, consider buying them at a local hardware store. Whether you are a beginner crafter or an expert, everyone should have them. And if you are like me, feel free to paint them a matching color.

Claw hammer

Phillips screwdriver

Drill

Sandpaper, varying from 100 to 220 grit

Industrial-strength wood glue

Safety goggles

1" chip paintbrush

2" chip paintbrush

2" slant paintbrush

Small flat and round craft paintbrushes

SAWS

There are four different kinds of saws I use when working with wood projects at home: chop saw, miter saw, table saw, and jigsaw.

The main difference between a chop saw and a miter saw is a miter saw can rotate and make angled cuts. These angled cuts are often referred to as "miters," hence the name. A chop saw only cuts straight, ninety-degree angles. A miter saw is traditionally attached to a base and often elevated on legs, and a chop saw is handheld. A cordless chop saw is my favorite tool when creating small DIY projects and furniture.

A table saw or saw bench is a circular saw where the blade protrudes through the surface of a table, which provides support for the wood being cut. It is driven by an electric motor and is a costly investment. I do not use a table saw in any of the projects in this book because it is an intimidating tool for beginners. I also do not recommend using one without first taking a class to better understand its proper safety and use. If you have a table saw and are comfortable using it, it's great for creating straight clean cuts in wood.

A jigsaw is probably the most versatile power tool you can own. It is made up of an electric motor and reciprocating saw blade. In addition to making straight and angle cuts, it is excellent for cutting curves. Like all the other power tools previously mentioned, be sure to get the proper training you need to understand how to use a jigsaw.

I primarily use a chop saw and a miter saw for these projects. They are less expensive tools and more portable than a table saw. I have found that when I take my time with a chop saw, I can achieve straight cuts.

Safety is key, so use what is the most comfortable and appropriate tool for each project. And be sure to wear safety goggles!

PAINT

I prefer acrylic brush-on paint for most projects. (Acrylic craft paint and latex paint are the same; both are water-based and made from acrylic resins. I prefer using the word *acrylic* because it is available in smaller craft sizes.) Water-based paints and stains tend to have low or no VOCs (volatile organic compounds) and can be safely used indoors or outdoors. Acrylic paint has a variety of sheens and finishes and can be found at craft and home improvement stores. More and more craft stores are selling paint in eight-ounce jars. Craft paint will work well with some of these projects too. I mostly use DecoArt Americana Decor paints because they are readily available in major retail stores and online. The Satin Enamels and Chalky Finish lines are among my favorites.

Wooden crates are made of very dry absorbent wood. When painting, you will most likely need to apply two to three coats to achieve the desired sheen and create the most durable finish.

VARNISH

Living in a busy home, I protect my projects with clear varnish. There are many water-based varnishes that are safe to use indoors and outdoors. They come in a variety of finishes, from flat matte to high gloss sheen. I prefer a satin finish for most of my projects and always use a gloss sheen for projects exposed to moisture. DuraClear is my favorite brand, and it comes in two- to eight-ounce sizes and can be found in craft stores.

PAINTBRUSHES

Paintbrushes come in all shapes and sizes, and for simple projects like these, inexpensive one-inch or two-inch chip brushes will suffice. They cost about one dollar each at home improvement stores. You can rewash and reuse the brushes when using water-based paint. Chip brushes are perfect for getting into those tight spaces wooden crates are famous for, and their rough bristles are ideal for techniques like dry brushing. For large scale projects, I often use a finer quality two-inch slant brush.

CRAFTING
WITH
WOODEN
CRATES & PALLETS

How to Build a Crate

Wooden crates are incredibly useful storage pieces, especially when you can customize your own. A standard crate measures 12½" x 18" x 9½", but it is often not quite the right size for what you need. By making small adjustments to the wood and slats, you can create the perfect storage piece for any space. Pine board works best, but you also can use cheaper plywood board. However, the plywood will have rougher edges once cut.

SUPPLIES YOU WILL NEED

- 6' long sheet of ¾" x 12" pine board
- ruler
- pencil
- saw
- 2½" balsa wood slats

- 220 grit sandpaper
- cotton cloth
- hammer
- ½" nails
- wood glue
- painter's tape

- acrylic craft paint in white, coral, and blue
- 2" chip paintbrush
- decorative cabinet hardware

1 Determine your crate size. I decided to make a 12" x 12" x 10" crate. Measure the pine board to create two 10" pieces and one 10½" piece for the bottom. Wooden crates often have slats on the bottom, but to make the crate sturdier, use a solid bottom piece. Be sure to have a ruler and pencil handy to draw straight lines for cutting.

2 Use a circular saw, chop saw, miter saw, or table saw to cut the pine board in two 10" pieces and one 10½" piece. Select the tool that works best for you.

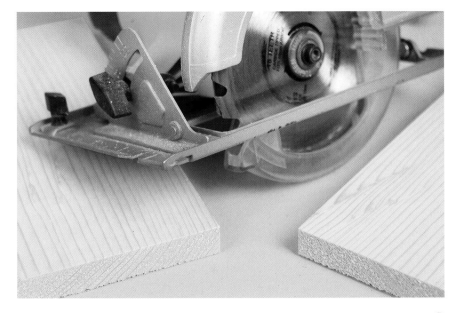

3 To create slats, use a ruler and pencil to measure nine pieces of balsa wood. You need three 12" slats for the left side and three 12" slats for the right side. Cut three 12" slats for the bottom if you prefer that over a solid wood piece.

4 Clean up uneven edges and areas and any other flaws from your cuts with sandpaper. When sanding, follow the direction of the wood grain. Carefully run your fingers over the surface when done to make sure you don't have any rough spots. Remove dust with a clean dry cloth.

5 With a hammer and nails, attach the crate base and sides together. Use wood glue for additional support, if needed. After assembling the sides to the base, place the crate on one side, lay down three slats evenly spaced apart, and attach them. Ideally, you want to use two nails on each side of the slats for maximum durability and strength. Balsa performs better with nails, not screws, because it is a delicate wood.

6 Repeating the same process in step 5, flip the crate to the other side and attach three slats.

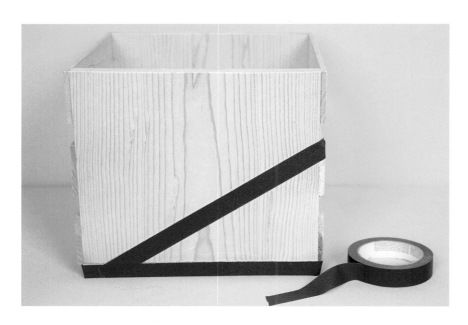

7 Using painter's tape, make a large triangle on the front of the crate. Press down firmly on the tape to create a good seal with the wood.

8 With white paint, paint inside the taped area with brushstrokes that follow the wood grain. Let the paint dry completely and add a second coat, if needed. Remove the painter's tape while the paint is still wet.

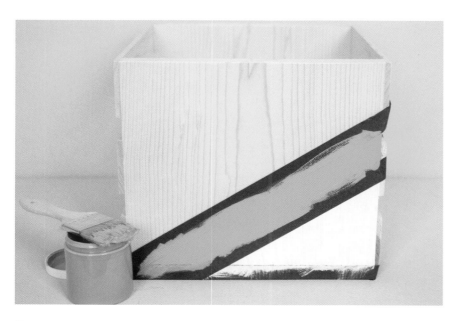

9 When the white paint is dry, put a second strip of painter's tape on the front of the crate. Paint one to two coats of coral paint, removing the tape while the second coat is still wet.

10 When the coral paint is completely dry, place a third strip of painter's tape on the front of the crate and paint one to two coats with blue paint. Remove tape before the paint is dry. Touch up any areas, if needed, with all three colors.

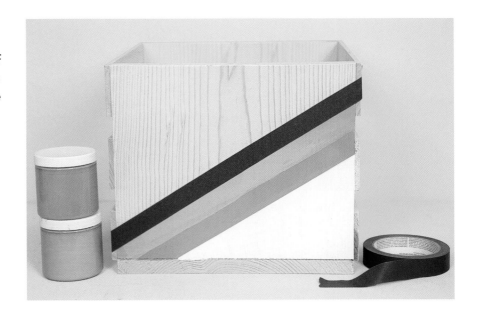

11 Attach decorative cabinet hardware. A drawer knob or a drawer pull is a perfect way to give your crate a little more personality.

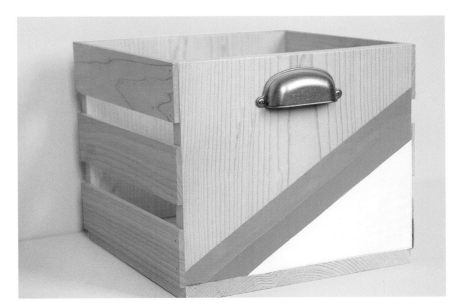

TIP

To adjust the size of the crate, increase the length of the bottom piece and slats to the desired size. You also can create traditional hand slots by using a jigsaw and 1" drill bit. To make a more durable heavy-duty crate, substitute balsa wood with 1" x 3" solid wood boards and substitute ½" nails with 1" screws.

Crate Storage Shelves

As wooden crates become more popular, manufacturers are building them in several different sizes. The crates I used for this project measure 10½" x 15" x 7½". I didn't want my storage shelves to be too deep, so this slightly smaller size was ideal. Use whatever size fits your needs. If you are using several crates to create wall storage, try mixing it up for a whimsical wall display.

SUPPLIES YOU WILL NEED

- two 10½" x 15" x 7½" wooden crates
- 220 grit sandpaper
- cotton cloth
- 2" chip paintbrush
- acrylic satin paint in blue and off-white
- two wood corbels (see page 10)
- two 2" metal mending plates
- ½" screws
- screwdriver
- two 1" L-shaped metal corner braces

1 Smooth any of the crates' rough edges with sandpaper because you will want the shelves to be easy to the touch. When done sanding, wipe away dust with a clean dry cloth.

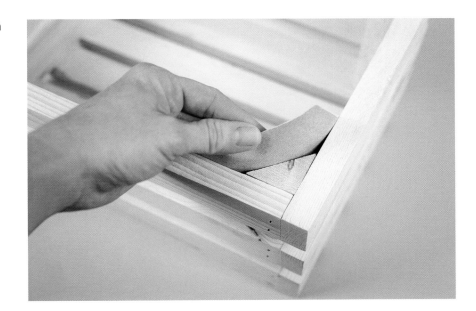

2 Using a paintbrush and blue paint, paint the crates with a thin coat, following the wood grain. It's easier to paint the inside first and then the outside. Let dry completely.

3 Apply a second coat of blue paint, if needed. Let the paint fully dry and cure before going to the next step.

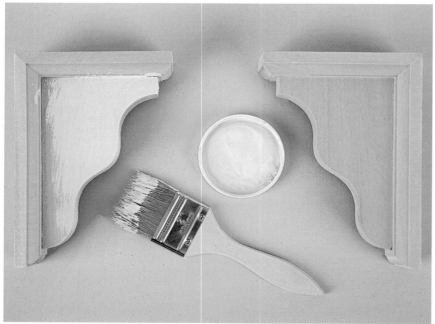

4 Paint the corbels with off-white paint. Let dry.

5 Apply a second coat of off-white paint on the corbels. Let dry completely.

6 Turn the crates over on to their back sides, laying them next to each other with the long sides together. Attach a mending plate near the top of the crates with two ½" screws and a screwdriver.

7 Rotate the crates and attach a second mending plate at the bottom with two ½" screws.

8 Use two L-shaped metal corner braces to attach the painted crates to a wall. Be sure to place the braces so that they screw into wall studs.

9 Attach the corbels to the wall directly underneath the crate storage shelves. The majority of the crates' weight should be supported by the corner braces at the top. The corbels provide additional support below.

10 Fill the crate storage shelves with your favorite display items. My shelves are in the bathroom and are the perfect place for extra hand towels.

TIP

Mending plates and corner braces are made of zinc-plated metal and are a great way to give support to wooden crate projects. They are inexpensive and can be found at home improvement stores. Since crates can be heavy, be sure to attach the braces to wall studs.

Hanging Crate Nightstands

Precious storage space can be hard to come by, especially in children's bedrooms. Go vertical with your storage by cutting wooden crates in half. These hanging crates make ideal nightstands and hold a lot of things in a small space.

SUPPLIES YOU WILL NEED

- 12½" x 18" x 9½" wooden crate
- pencil
- ruler
- jigsaw
- 100 grit sandpaper
- 220 grit sandpaper
- cotton cloth
- 2" chip paintbrush
- acrylic satin paint in yellow and blue
- decorative stencil
- white acrylic craft paint
- makeup sponges
- ½" screws
- screwdriver
- four metal mending plates

1 Lay the crate upside down. Use a pencil and ruler to measure 5" sections on both sides. Repeat on the other side. (For deeper storage, measure the crate to be cut in half.)

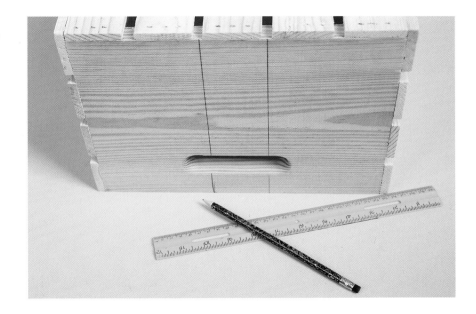

2 Carefully cut along the penciled lines with a jigsaw. You will have three pieces when done. The two sides will be your storage crates, and the middle piece can be discarded or saved for another project.

3 Smooth rough areas with 100 grit sandpaper. Go back with 220 grit sandpaper and soften the cut lines. Use a clean dry cloth to wipe away the dust.

4 With a paintbrush, paint one to two coats of yellow acrylic satin paint on one of the pieces. Let dry completely.

5 Paint one to two coats of blue acrylic satin paint on the other piece. Let dry completely.

6 Leave each crate as is or paint a fun pattern, using a decorative stencil and white acrylic craft paint.

7 Makeup sponges are ideal to paint without the stencil lines bleeding through, so use it to apply the white paint with the stencil.

8 Carefully remove the stencil while the paint is still wet. Allow the paint to dry before moving the stencil to another area to paint.

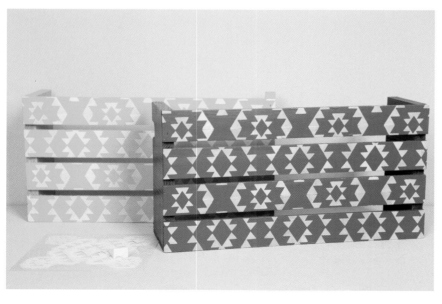

9 Stenciling can be tedious and time-consuming, but the results are a gratifying way to create a unique piece for your home! Be sure to clean the stencil with mild soap and water when done.

10 With screws and a screwdriver, attach two metal mending plates to the back top area of each of the crates. Add two more mending plates at the bottom for additional support, if needed.

11 Attach the crates to a wall in a vertical pattern and fill them with books and other favorite items.

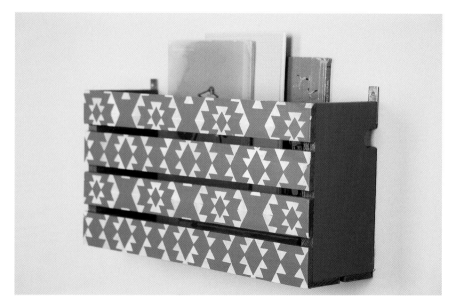

CRATE BOOKSHELF

Until I made my first piece of furniture with wooden crates, I never would have believed how sturdy and resilient they are. Besides being easy to assemble, crate pieces can be made incredibly strong by using metal mending plates. Metal top plates also can be used to create durable extensions and legs. Give this project a try, and you will be surprised how versatile it is!

SUPPLIES YOU WILL NEED

- four 12½" x 18" x 9½" wooden crates
- acrylic chalk paint in white, green, and yellow
- 2" chip paintbrush
- four wood furniture legs
- 220 grit sandpaper
- cotton cloth
- twelve metal mending plates
- ½" screws
- screwdriver
- wood glue
- four heavy-duty top plates
- ¾" screws
- two scrap pallet wood pieces 5½" x 25½"

1 Using white acrylic chalk paint and a paintbrush, paint the four furniture legs, following the direction of the wood grain.

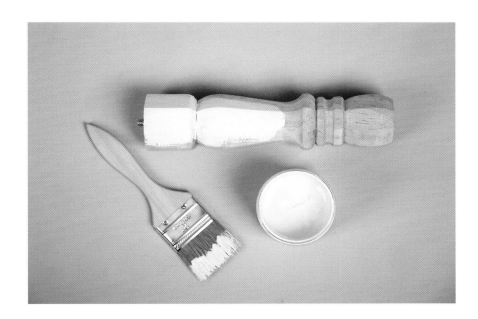

2 Apply a second coat of white paint on the legs, if needed. Chalk paint is very thick and may only need to be used a second time in some areas.

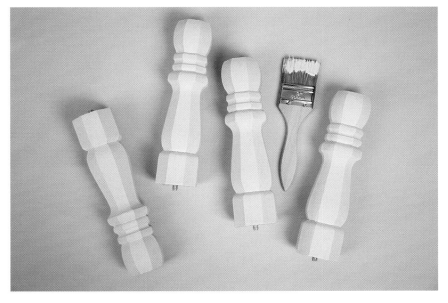

3 Smooth any rough areas on the four crates with sandpaper. Use a clean dry cloth to wipe away dust.

4 Paint the crates with green acrylic chalk paint, following the direction of the wood grain. Paint the inside first and then the outside. Let dry.

5 Apply a second coat of green paint, if needed.

6 Turn two crates over and lay them vertically, side-by-side. Attach two metal mending plates to the top and two plates to the bottom, using ½" screws and a screwdriver. Repeat this process on the second pair of crates.

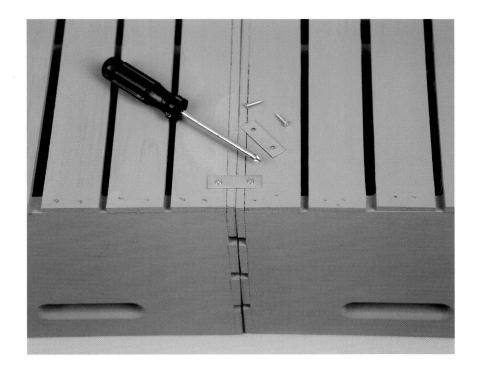

7 Set the two pairs of crates on top of each other and use two mending plates on each side to attach all four pieces together. Use wood glue for additional strength, if needed. Crates can sometimes vary slightly in size, so line them up as best as you can so that the bookshelf is level.

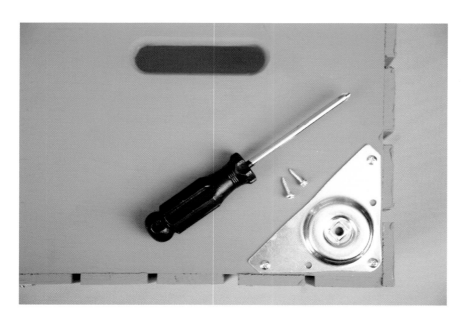

8 Turn the bookshelf upside down and attach the four heavy-duty top plates, using ¾" screws.

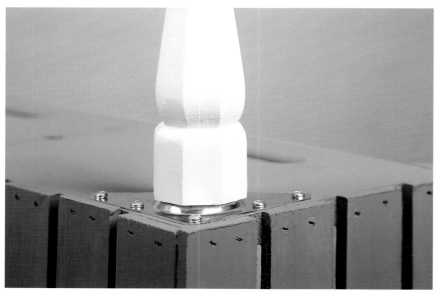

9 Place one wood leg on top and tightly screw it into place. Repeat with the other three legs.

10 Using two pieces of scrap pallet wood, cut them down to 5½" x 25½". Use sandpaper to smooth any rough or uneven areas.

11 Paint both pieces of scrap pallet wood, front and back, with yellow acrylic chalk paint. Let dry.

12 Glue both scrap pallet wood pieces to the top of the bookshelf. The wood pieces will hang slightly over the front and the sides. Let the glue dry completely before use.

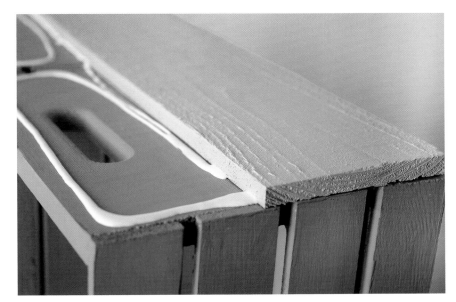

TIP

Chalk paint is fabulous for large-scale projects. Its matte finish dries quickly and can often be painted in a single coat. It is also easy to mix to create custom colors!

CRATE FOOTSTOOL

With two teenagers at home, "Movie Night" is a weekly occurrence. Everyone loves a cozy blanket when watching a flick, but the throw blankets strewn everywhere afterward become a nuisance. This unique storage solution not only provides more space for throws, it creates a cozy footstool too! For your fabric, find a flea market coffee bean bag or cover it with your favorite upholstery. Use whatever matches your home decor and personal style.

SUPPLIES YOU WILL NEED

- 12½" x 18" x 9½" wooden crate
- 220 grit sandpaper
- cotton cloth
- 2" chip paintbrush
- brown wood stain
- upholstery foam cushion

- scissors
- 3' x 4' Masonite board
- chop saw
- burlap sack
- fabric glue
- two zinc-plated metal hinges

- screwdriver
- ½" screws
- ¼" screws
- four 2" swivel plate casters

1 Prep the crate by smoothing any rough areas with sandpaper. Wipe away dust with a clean dry cloth.

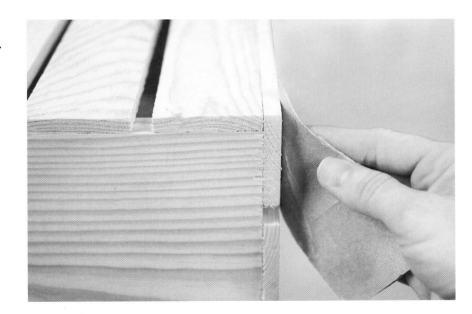

2 Using a paintbrush, paint the stain in long even strokes following the wood grain.

3 While the stain is still wet, wipe it back using a clean dry cloth. You can layer stain by repeating the process for a darker look. For a light stain, brush and wipe back once. Because crates have so many nooks and crannies, you will need to apply the stain first with a brush before wiping it back in most areas.

4 While the stain dries, cut the upholstery foam cushion to 12½" x 18" with scissors.

5 Measure the Masonite board to 12½" x 18" and use a chop saw to cut to size. Place the cushion on top.

6 Wrap burlap sack around the cushion and Masonite board.

7 Pull burlap corners tight and adhere in place with fabric glue. Let dry. Trim any remaining excess fabric.

8 Attach two metal hinges near the edge of the crate sides, using a screwdriver and ½" screws on the wood side and ¼" screws on the cushion side.

9 Open and close to make sure the cushion lays flat. Be sure to attach your hinges, so the rounded side faces out.

10 Using ½" screws, attach the four swivel plate casters to the bottom of the crate.

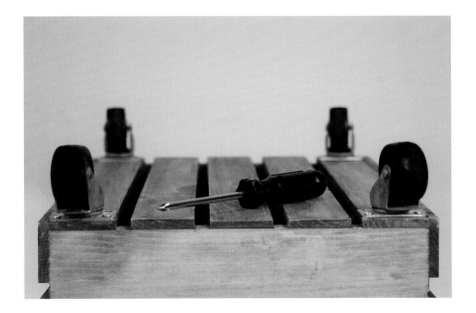

11 Turn the crate right side up and check to make sure the casters work properly. I did not use locking casters so that my footstool will swivel freely on carpet. You may want to consider casters that lock in place for slick or wood floors.

TIP

There's no need to distress your crate if you can find one already done for you. A vintage fruit or vegetable crate makes a great predistressed solution. Just be sure to clean and seal the wood with a water-based varnish before use.

CRATE SIDE TABLE

A crate side table is definitely a resourceful way to save money and create a unique piece of furniture. You can turn the crate vertical or horizontal, depending on your desired height, and furniture legs are a fun and inexpensive way to give your table some personality.

SUPPLIES YOU WILL NEED

- 12½" x 18" x 9½" wooden crate
- 220 grit sandpaper
- cotton cloth
- 2" chip paintbrush
- acrylic paint in green, silver, and blue
- four wood furniture legs
- painter's tape
- four metal top plates
- screwdriver
- ¾" screws
- furniture pads

1 Smooth any rough areas of the crate with sandpaper. Wipe away dust with a clean dry cloth.

2 Using a paintbrush, paint the entire crate green, working from the inside out. Let dry.

3 Apply a second coat of green paint. Let dry and cure completely.

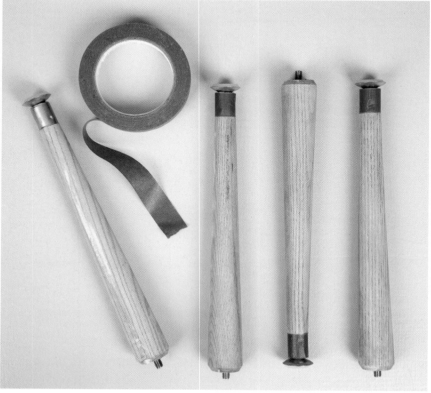

4 While the paint is drying, prep the table legs by taping off the foot areas you do not want to paint.

5 Using a paintbrush, apply a thin coat of silver paint on one side of each leg. Let dry.

6 Rotate and paint the back side of each leg with the same silver paint. Let dry. Touch up any areas, if needed. Metallic paint sheen performs best when painted in the same direction.

7 Lay the painted crate on one side. Using painter's tape, tape half of the crate from one corner to the other. Press tape down firmly to create a strong seal.

8 Using blue paint, paint one side of the surface, being careful not to get any in between the slats. Let dry.

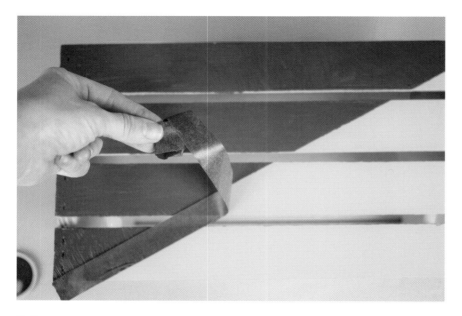

9 Apply a second coat of blue paint, if needed, and carefully remove the painter's tape while the paint is still wet. Touch up any areas and let dry.

10 Turn the crate upside down. In each of the four corners, attach a metal top plate, using a screwdriver and ¾" screws.

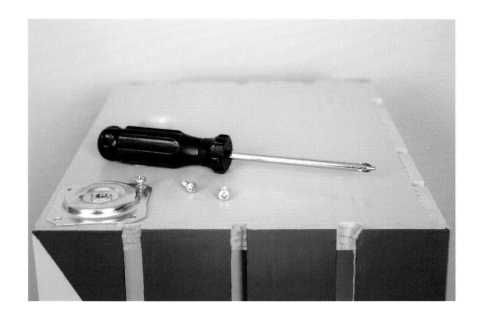

11 Gently screw in legs until they are snug. Be sure to add furniture pads to the bottoms to protect floors.

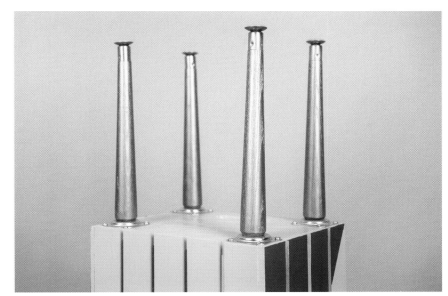

TIP

You can't find the legs you are looking for? An old piece of furniture at a thrift store might have just the ones you want! Try "upcycling" an old find to create the ideal piece to fit your needs.

CRATE BENCH

We recently moved, leaving behind a home with a glorious oversize mudroom. Our new house lacked sufficient shoe storage. After many attempts to keep our footwear in various containers, I realized something a little more stylish would motivate us to keep them organized. This simple bench, made from two wooden crates, ended up being the perfect solution!

SUPPLIES YOU WILL NEED

- two ¾" x 11¼" x 38" pine boards
- 220 grit sandpaper
- cotton cloth
- 2" chip paintbrush
- semigloss acrylic paint in white, gray, and metallic-blue
- two 12½" x 18" x 9½" wooden crates
- four 5" wood fence post tops
- two metal mending plates
- screwdriver
- ½" screws
- wood glue
- hammer
- 1" nails
- drill
- ¼" drill bit

1 Smooth pine boards with sandpaper to eliminate any rough areas. Wipe away dust with a clean dry cloth.

2 Using a paintbrush, paint both boards white, front and back, following the wood grain. Let dry. Apply a second coat of white paint, if needed.

3 While the boards dry, sand any rough areas on the crates. Wipe away dust with a clean dry cloth.

4 Paint both crates with gray paint, working from the inside out. Let dry.

5 Apply a second coat of gray paint, if needed. Let dry completely.

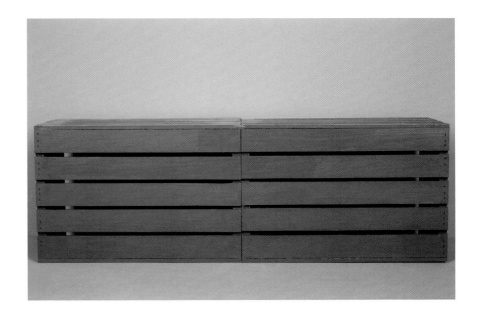

6 While the crates dry, paint the fence post tops, which will serve as bench legs, with metallic-blue paint. Let dry. Apply a second coat of metallic-blue paint, if needed. Be careful not to paint the screws attached to the tops.

7 Once the crates are dry, attach two mending plates to the back side with a screwdriver and ½" screws. For extra durability, use wood glue.

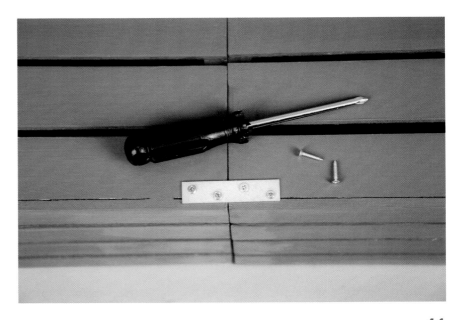

8 Turn the crate bench upside down. Use a hammer and nails to attach one of the white boards as the bottom. Be sure to center the crates in the middle of the board.

9 Using a drill and ¼" drill bit, make a hole in each corner. Fill with wood glue, and screw in the fence post tops. Let dry completely.

10 Flip bench right side up and use a hammer and nails to attach the other white board as the top. Again, be sure to center the crates on the board. Fill and paint nail holes, if desired.

11 Place the bench in desired area and fill with shoes!

TIP

I recommend a semigloss or gloss finish for this project, if it will be in a high-traffic area. If you are not able to find gloss metallic paint, use a water-based gloss varnish.

Kids' Crate Storage

I have creative children, and each one has a vast amount of materials they love to use when making things. We needed something where they could see their supplies and keep them neatly organized. This crate storage ended up being the perfect solution! The shelves help keep supplies on hand, and the clear containers make them visible and easy to access.

Supplies You Will Need

- three 12½" x 18" x 9½" wooden crates
- hammer
- pliers
- 220 grit sandpaper
- cotton cloth
- painter's tape
- 2" chip paintbrush
- gold acrylic paint
- green spray paint
- four 1¼" x 48" zinc-plated punched angle brackets
- screwdriver
- ½" screws and washers
- furniture pads

1 With a hammer, gently remove the top two slats on one side of each of the three crates. You should be able to do this with a few taps. Be sure to get rid of any nails or staples left behind with pliers.

2 Smooth any rough areas with sandpaper. Wipe away dust with a clean dry cloth.

3 Lay the crate on its side with the missing slats facing right. Place a long piece of painter's tape from the top left corner to the bottom right corner. Press down firmly for a good seal.

4 Use your paintbrush and gold paint to paint the left side of the crate (not the wood slats). Let dry. Add a second coat of gold paint, if needed. For the best sheen, follow the wood grain and paint in one direction.

5 Use the green spray paint to color the inside of the zinc-plated punched angle brackets. Be sure to spray outdoors in a well-ventilated area. Let dry overnight.

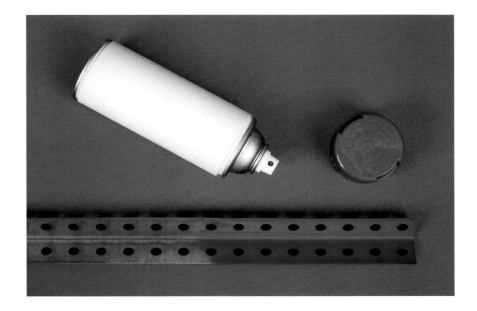

6 Flip the brackets over and spray the back side. Let dry completely. Flip over again and touch up any areas as needed. Repeat on the back side. Make sure paint has dried to a nontacky finish before moving on to the next step.

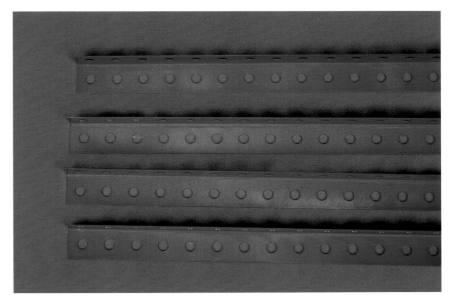

7 Lay the crates and brackets on the ground in desired pattern. I started six inches from the bottom of the brackets to create "legs." Using a screwdriver and ½" screws and washers, attach the brackets to the first crate on the bottom of each of the four sides.

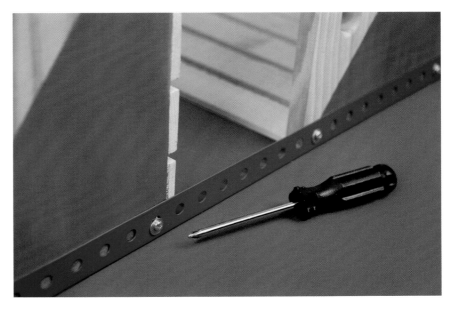

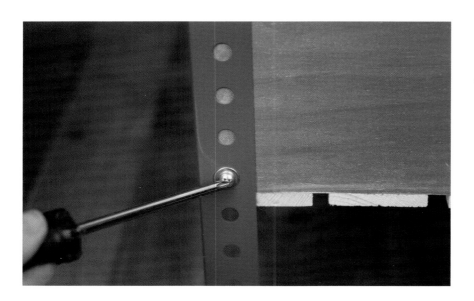

8 Repeat step 7 for the second and third crates, attaching the brackets on the bottoms of each of the four sides.

9 Stand the crates right side up and attach screws and washers to the top of each crate. Check the bottom crate and legs to make sure the entire structure is level. For indoor use, attach furniture pads on the bottom of the legs to protect your floors.

10

Use clear containers to fill and store your children's favorite supplies!

······················ **TIP** ······················

If you are making multiple versions of this crate, use different colors of spray paint to customize each one. This is a handy piece for a closet, pantry, or garage.

CRATE DESK

My oldest daughter started college and needed a desk in her room that fit a lot of books and supplies. Not wanting to purchase something that would be hard to move at the end of the school year, this crate desk was the perfect solution. Not only does it have ample space for school items, it's easy to take apart and move year after year.

SUPPLIES YOU WILL NEED

- four 12½" x 18" x 9½" wooden crates
- two 12½" x 27" x 9½" wooden crates
- 24" x 48" x ¾" plywood
- 220 grit sandpaper
- cotton cloth

- 2" chip paintbrush
- acrylic chalk paint in coral and blue
- eight 2" metal mending plates
- screwdriver
- ½" screws
- clear varnish (optional)

1 Smooth any rough areas on the six crates and plywood with sandpaper. Use a clean dry cloth to wipe away any dust.

2 Using coral paint, paint the inside of two of the smaller crates. Try to paint just the surface and not in between the slats. Let dry.

3 Once the coral paint is completely dry, use sandpaper to clean up any areas that were painted outside the surface. I use chalk paint because it is easy to sand off.

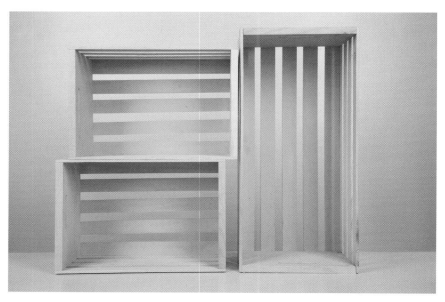

4 Repeat steps 2 and 3 on one of the larger crates, so you have two small crates and one large crate painted in coral.

5 Using the blue paint, paint the inside of the remaining two smaller crates. Again, try to paint just the surface, not in between the slats. Let dry.

6 Once the blue paint is completely dry, use sandpaper to clean up any areas that were painted outside the surface.

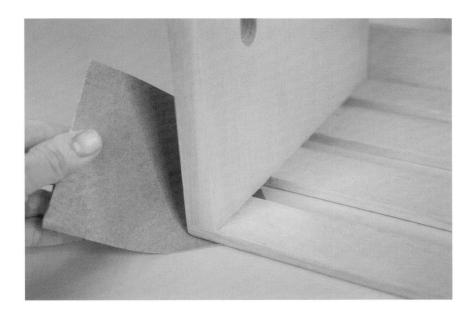

7 Repeat steps 5 and 6 on the second large crate, so you have two small crates and one large crate painted in blue. Let all the crates dry and cure completely.

8 Set the two large crates upright vertically. Place the plywood on top, so it is aligned with the back side of the crates and hanging over the right and left sides, approximately two inches. Using mending plates, a screwdriver, and ½" screws, adhere the crate on the right side to the desktop.

9 Repeat adhering the crate on the left side with mending plates, a screwdriver, and ½" screws, so both crates are attached to the desktop.

10 Place a small crate horizontally on top of the right-hand side of the desktop, aligning it to the back and side edges. Use a mending plate to attach it in place.

11 Repeat step 10 on the left side. Be sure to use different color crates on opposite sides of each other. Add more mending plates to the back side for additional security.

12 Add the remaining two crates to the tops of the smaller crates, using two to four mending plates as needed. (Do not use wood glue because it will prohibit you later on from taking apart the desk.) Once you are done with the assembly, fill the desk with your favorite things and school supplies!

· TIP ·

Leave the desktop raw or seal it with a varnish for extra durability. I recommend a matte or satin water-based varnish if you want to keep the look of unfinished wood.

Crate Pet Bed

Our friend adopted a dog, and we thought of the perfect do-it-yourself gift to welcome her home: a new pet bed! An oversize crate is a fabulous option for helping an animal adjust to its new space. The crate has ample room for a cushion and is easy to climb in and out of. You can personalize the pet's new bed with a cute sign displaying its name!

SUPPLIES YOU WILL NEED

- 12½" x 27" x 9½" wooden crate
- hammer
- pliers
- 100 grit and 220 grit sandpaper
- cotton cloth
- 2" chip paintbrush

- acrylic paint in blue and off-white
- 8" x 12" oval wood plaque
- pencil
- graphite transfer paper
- small round craft paintbrush

- 2" x 2" x 36" wood
- miter saw
- wood glue
- upholstery foam cushion
- 1 yard fabric

1 Gently remove the top two slats on one side of the crate with a hammer. You should be able to take them off with a few gentle taps. Use pliers to remove any nails or staples that remain.

2 You don't want your sweet pet to get any wood slivers, so use 100 grit sandpaper to smooth any rough edges. Go over the entire surface with 220 grit sandpaper when done. Wipe away dust with a clean dry cloth.

3 Using a 2" chip paintbrush, apply blue paint to the inside of the slats, being careful not to get paint in between.

4 Lay the crate on its side. Carefully paint the inside area blue, avoiding in between the slats. Flip the crate over and paint the other inside area blue. Let dry completely. Apply a second coat, if needed.

5 When the paint is completely dried and cured, use 220 grit sandpaper to clean up edges where the paint spilled over. The sandpaper will help create crisp smooth edges.

6 Set aside the crate and color both sides of the plaque with off-white paint, using a 2" chip paintbrush. Add a second coat, if needed.

7 Print a pattern that you want to use on the plaque, and get a pencil and graphite transfer paper.

8 Place the graphite transfer paper underneath the pattern and on top of the plaque. With pencil to paper, transfer the text to the plaque's surface, creating a template to paint.

9 With a small round craft paintbrush, paint within the transfer lines. Or you can skip steps 7 and 8 and customize a sign with your own hand-lettering!

10 To create legs for the pet bed, cut the 2" x 2" x 36" wood into four 6" pieces with a miter saw.

11 Smooth the legs with 220 grit sandpaper.

12 Use industrial-strength wood glue to attach each leg to the base of the pet bed. Let it dry completely. Reinforce with wood screws for a larger animal.

13 Cut the upholstery foam cushion down to 11½" x 25". Cover with fabric, neatly tucking it underneath, and insert it in the pet bed. A twin sheet, cut down, is a superb solution because it can be removed easily and washed on a regular basis.

For the safety of your pet, do not leave the pet bed in an unattended area, if you think your animal might chew on it. Use waterproof fabric for a pet that has frequent accidents.

VINTAGE SODA CRATE STORAGE

Vintage soda crates are fun to collect and use for storage. They originally were made to house bottles of all shapes and sizes, which resulted in lots of neat dividers and inserts. Try to find an assortment of colors and styles for a whimsical display. They come in all different conditions, and it is not uncommon for them to need some serious repair. Below you will find several tips to clean, fix, and protect your vintage soda crates.

SUPPLIES YOU WILL NEED

- three vintage soda crates measuring around 4" x 12" x 18"

- cotton cloth

- 2" chip paintbrush

- water-based matte varnish

- oil-based varnish

- 100 grit sandpaper

- 220 grit sandpaper

- Masonite board

- wood glue

- screwdriver

- ½" screws

- six 1" zinc-plated corner brackets

- 1½" screws

1 For crates in good condition, use a clean dry cloth to wipe away dust. Use mild soap and water for any spills and dirt. Let dry completely before moving on to the next step.

2 Use water-based matte varnish to seal and protect the crates. This will prevent wear and tear. If you notice any rust on the hardware, use an oil-based varnish to seal it and keep it from rusting further.

3 For crates that are structurally sound but have excessive amounts of chipping paint, use 100 grit sandpaper to remove the paint chips.

4 After removing the paint chips, go back with 220 grit sandpaper and smooth any rough areas. You can determine how much paint you want to remove. When done, use matte varnish to seal the entire surface.

5 For crates in really bad shape, remove and repair any splinters or broken pieces. Replace large damaged areas with Masonite board.

6 For small damaged areas, use industrial-strength wood glue to reattach broken pieces. Let the glue dry for twenty-four hours before proceeding. Once dry, lightly sand the area with 220 grit sandpaper and use matte varnish to seal the surface.

7 Vintage soda crates often have bent or broken hardware. Remove it entirely, or use new screws and wood glue to reattach it. For excessive hardware damage, use epoxy-strength glue.

8 Once all the crates have been repaired and sealed with matte varnish, attach two zinc-plated corner brackets to the top of each crate with a screwdriver and ½" screws. Determine whether you will be hanging the crates vertically or horizontally before attaching the brackets.

9 Attach the corner brackets to a wall, using 1½" screws drilled into a wood stud or drywall screws. Two brackets at the top of each crate should suffice, though more can be added at the bottom to help support heavy items.

10 Fill the crates with your favorite craft items! Vintage soda crates are also great for kitchen pantry storage, displaying photo frames, and even hanging in a closet for purses and accessories!

TIP

Search local flea markets and antique stores for vintage soda crates. You can't find what you are looking for? Try cutting a new crate down to a similar size and painting it in vintage-like colors.

Crate Plant Stand

Vintage fruit and vegetable crates are easy to find at flea markets, antique stores, and online. Be sure to check the stability and smell of a crate before purchasing it. One that has been stored near someone who smokes or next to gasoline in a garage won't work. Varnish, however, can help with musty scents as long as the wood is completely dry. A vintage crate in excellent shape can easily be had for under twenty dollars, so keep an eye out for a great find!

SUPPLIES YOU WILL NEED

- vintage fruit or vegetable crate measuring 14" x 18" x 10"
- wood glue
- hammer
- ¾" nails
- 1" nails
- 220 grit sandpaper
- cotton cloth
- water-based satin varnish
- paintbrush
- four new or used wood banisters
- pencil
- ruler
- chop saw
- 100 grit sandpaper

1 If using a vintage crate, be sure to repair any damaged areas with wood glue. Check all the slats to make sure they are firmly in place. Add additional nail supports, if needed, and make certain the crate is completely dry before crafting.

2 After giving the crate a thorough check, use 220 grit sandpaper to smooth rough areas and splinters. When done, wipe the crate with a clean dry cloth.

3 Use varnish to seal the entire surface, working from the inside out. Let it fully dry and cure. Apply a second coat of varnish, if the plant stand will be placed outside.

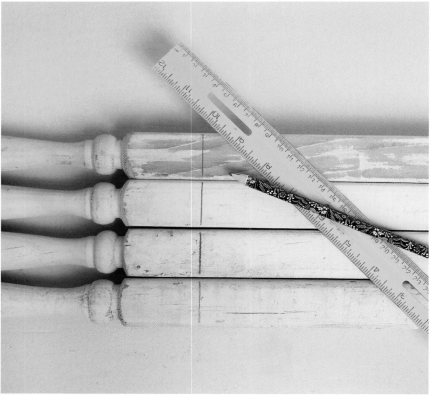

4 Measure one side of the wood banisters and draw cut lines at 24" long.

5 With a chop saw, cut the banisters evenly along the cut lines. Vintage banisters might be slightly uneven, so be sure to saw them at the same length even if the style is different.

6 Using 220 grit sandpaper, smooth the cut area of the banisters and any spots that feel rough or uneven.

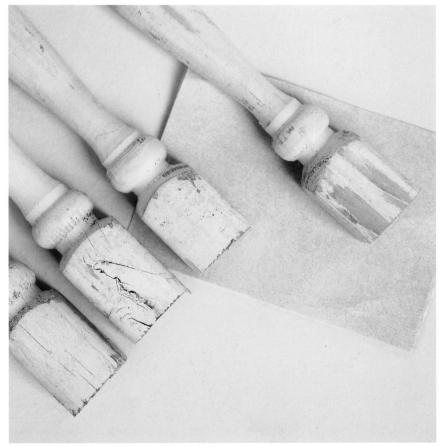

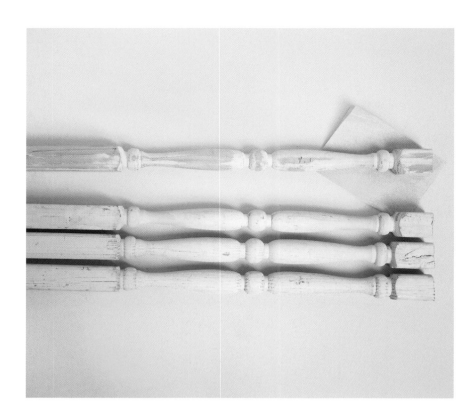

7 For vintage banisters, sand any chipping paint for an added distressed feel. For new banisters, paint them with chalk paint and a clear wax varnish. Once dry, sand back with 100 grit sandpaper to expose raw areas of the wood for a distressed look.

8 Lay the crate on its side and attach the banisters, using four ¾" nails on each leg and hammering one through each slat. Make sure to attach the legs with the cut-side down.

9 Turn the crate right side up and use ¾" or 1" nails to attach the banister legs from the top. Check the stability of the crate and add additional nails or glue, if needed.

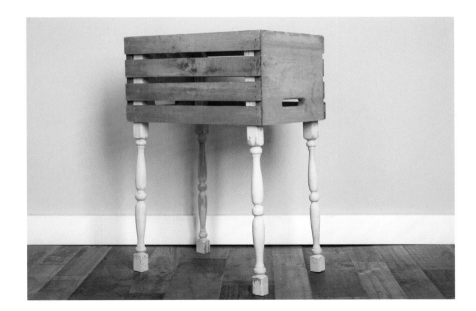

10 Give the tabletop a second coat of varnish. Since the plant stand may have water spilled on it, you want to be confident the wood is protected from moisture. Place your plants in waterproof containers or in pots with saucers to prevent spilling.

TIP

If you have a green thumb, create several more plant stands of varying heights. Paint them different colors for a bright and colorful display.

VINTAGE CRATE FAIRY GARDEN

Old or new, a wooden crate is the perfect raised garden for your fantasy fairy friends! You can find inexpensive dollhouse furniture in local craft stores, and combined with a few rocks and plants, you'll have the perfect magical retreat. This is a fun project to do with children and makes a perfect housewarming gift for a friend.

SUPPLIES YOU WILL NEED

- vintage soda crate measuring 4" x 12" x 18"
- 220 grit sandpaper
- cotton cloth
- 2" chip paintbrush
- waterproof gloss varnish
- small round craft paintbrush
- craft paint in red, white, and coral
- dollhouse furniture
- scissors
- colorful craft paper
- string
- wood skewers
- craft glue
- plastic trash bag
- potting soil
- plants
- wood slices
- pebbles
- rocks

1 Prep the crate by using sandpaper to smooth any chipping paint or uneven surfaces. When done, wipe down with a clean dry cloth.

2 Seal the crate, inside and outside, using 2" chip paintbrush and waterproof gloss varnish. Let dry completely.

3 Paint dollhouse furniture with small round craft paintbrush. I used red craft paint for chairs, white for a fence, and coral for a gazebo.

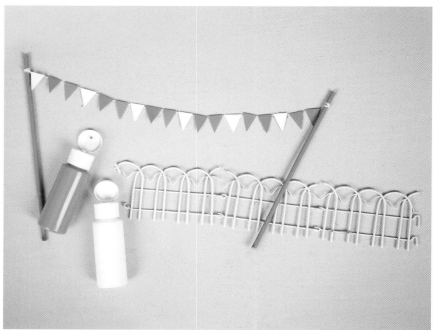

4 Using scissors and colorful craft paper, cut tiny ½" triangle pennants. Attach them to string and wood skewers with craft glue. Paint skewers with small round craft paintbrush and coral paint.

5 Measure the inside of the crate and use scissors to cut a plastic trash bag to size. You want it to cover and protect the bottom and sides of the crate. For my 4" x 12" x 18" crate, I cut a piece measuring 16" x 22".

6 Center the plastic bag in the middle of the crate. Carefully align the sides and cover most of the inside.

7 To help hold the plastic in place, fill the crate with potting soil. Add enough dirt until it reaches up to ½" from the top.

8 Place plants inside the crate in desired locations. The type of plants you use will vary, depending on how much sun the fairy garden will get. Ask a local nursery for help choosing plants.

9 Insert painted furniture and fence in the crate. Use small wood slices and pebbles to create a whimsical walking path.

10 Place a few larger rocks in corner areas, depending on how much space you want to fill.

11 Insert skewers with pennants and remainder of decorations. Carefully water plants, and place the fairy garden indoors or outdoors.

TIP

Change out the furniture for different seasons. Add small pumpkins for fall and a bottle brush tree for Christmas. Have fun, and good luck catching a fairy or two!

CRATE LEMONADE STAND

I have four children, so lemonade stands always have been part of our lives. Every summer we pull out a folding table and make handmade signs. My kids were thrilled at the idea of building our own permanent structure, and using wooden crates turned what could have been an entire weekend project into a short afternoon. I couldn't believe we had a lemonade stand—assembled, painted, and decorated—in a few hours.

SUPPLIES YOU WILL NEED

- 1" x 3" x 64" wood furring strip
- miter saw
- 220 grit sandpaper
- four 12½" x 18" x 9½" wooden crates
- cotton cloth
- 2" paintbrush
- acrylic paint in white, coral, & yellow

- wood glue
- five 2" zinc-plated mending plates
- ½" screws
- screwdriver
- 9" x 12" wood sign
- four 2" swivel plate casters
- 1" screws

- decorative cabinet hardware
- felt balls and paper garland (optional)
- graphite transfer paper
- pencil
- small round craft paintbrush

1 Cut the wood furring strip in half, creating two 32" pieces. Lightly sand the entire surface and cut lines with sandpaper.

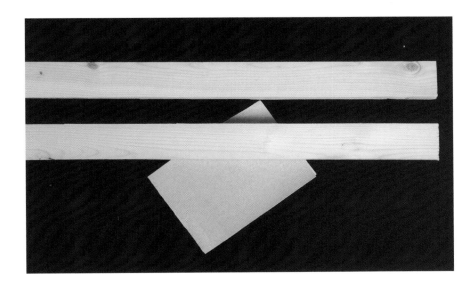

2 Prep the four crates by sanding any rough areas. Wipe away dust with a clean dry cloth.

3 Paint both sides of the furring strips with 2" paintbrush and white acrylic paint. Let dry. Apply a second coat, if needed.

4 Paint the four crates with white paint, starting with the inside and working your way out. Let dry.

5 Apply a second coat of white paint on the crates, if needed. Let dry. Stack crates in desired arrangement.

6 Adhere crates together using wood glue, mending plates, and ½" screws. Use one mending plate in the center and four more where each crate meets on the back side. Paint mending plates white, if desired.

7 While the wood glue dries, prep the sign by painting both sides with coral paint. Let dry. Apply a second coat, if needed.

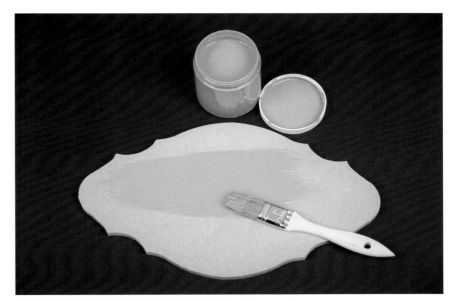

8 Turn the crates facing forward. Paint the top, fifth, and ninth slats with yellow paint, being careful not to get paint in between the slats. Let dry. Apply a second coat, if needed.

9 Using coral paint, paint the third and seventh slats, being careful not to get paint in between the slats. Let dry. Add a second coat, if needed.

10 Turn lemonade stand upside down. Attach casters on the bottom in each corner, using 1" screws.

11 Turn crate right side up. Attach furring strips to each side with 1" screws. String paper garland along the top as shown here, and add felt balls if you like.

12 Print a Lemonade sign that you want to use. Transfer design using graphite transfer paper and pencil.

13 Paint transferred lettering using a small round craft paintbrush and white paint. Let dry. Hang on front of lemonade stand.

TIP

When not selling lemonade, use the festive stand for your next party! It is the perfect surface for holding desserts, drinks, and paper products, and the casters make the stand easy to move.

CRATE PLANTER BOX

I love the look of a planter box on a front porch or back deck. A planter box can be expensive, so why not create a colorful statement piece for your outdoor decor by adding simple legs and a painted pattern to an existing wooden crate?

SUPPLIES YOU WILL NEED

- 2" x 2" x 24" wood
- pencil
- ruler
- miter saw
- 220 grit sandpaper
- cotton cloth
- 9½" x 15" x 7¼" wooden crate
- water-based coral wood stain
- 2" paintbrush
- wood glue
- 1" painter's tape
- white acrylic paint
- ½" craft paintbrush

1 Start by making the legs. Measure and cut the 2" x 2" x 24" wood into four 6" pieces with a miter saw.

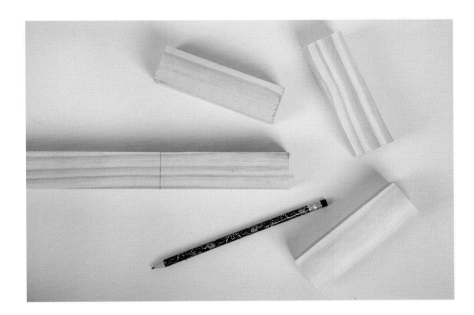

2 Smooth the legs along the cut lines and edges with sandpaper, creating an even surface. Wipe away dust with a clean dry cloth.

3 Sand the crate, smoothing out any rough edges. Wipe away dust with a clean dry cloth.

4 Using the coral wood stain and 2" paintbrush, paint the crate exterior.

5 Use a clean dry cloth to wipe away excess stain.

6 Repeat steps 4 and 5, working over the entire surface of the crate and between slats. Let dry completely.

7 Brush stain on legs and wipe away excess stain. Let dry.

8 Adhere legs, using industrial-strength wood glue. If the planter box is going outdoors, make sure the wood glue is water-resistant. Let dry.

9 Using painter's tape, tape off a stripe pattern around all four sides of the crate. Press tape firmly to create a good seal.

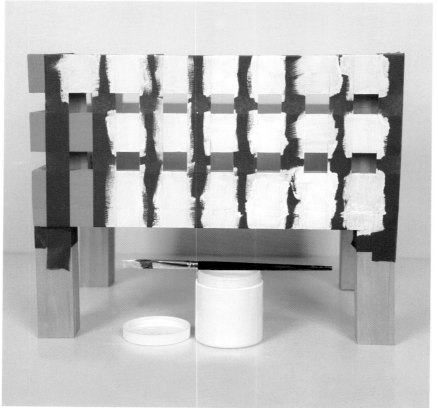

10 On one side of the crate, use white acrylic paint and ½" craft paintbrush to paint in between taped areas.

11 Remove tape while paint is still wet. Repeat on remaining three sides of the crate.

12 Let paint fully dry and cure. Touch up any areas as needed.

TIP

Place potted plants inside the planter box for full display. For more permanent plants, adhere plastic inside the box, so soil and plants can be directly added to each one.

HANGING FLOWERS PALLET

Pallet wood used to be difficult to take apart, but now you can find pallets that are easy to use for craft projects. These pallets come without all the rough broken wood and slivers and are not sprayed with harsh chemicals. The one pictured here is one-fourth the size of a traditional pallet and comes ready to craft!

SUPPLIES YOU WILL NEED

- pallet measuring 23" x 20" x 5"
- 220 grit sandpaper
- cotton cloth
- chalk paint in yellow and white
- 2" chip paintbrush
- two sawtooth frame hangers
- screwdriver
- ¼" screws
- measuring tape
- pencil
- three cabinet hardware knobs
- drill
- ³⁄₁₆" drill bit
- pliers
- three Mason jars
- three Mason jar hanging brackets
- painter's tape
- ¼" flat craft paintbrush
- two potted flowers or plants

1   Lightly go over the pallet with sandpaper and make sure the wood is smooth. Wipe away dust with a clean dry cloth.

2   Using yellow chalk paint and 2" chip paintbrush, paint the front side of the pallet. Let dry.

3 Turn the pallet over and paint the back side with yellow chalk paint. Let dry.

4 While the pallet is turned on its back side, attach the sawtooth frame hangers on the top slat with a screwdriver and screws. Attach one on each end about ½" from the edge or at the approximate distance of your wall studs.

5 Use a measuring tape and pencil to mark where you want to attach the cabinet hardware knobs. Mine are about 5¾" apart and 2" from the top.

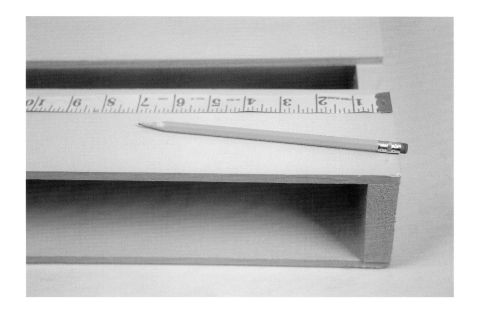

6 Drill holes for the knobs, using a drill and drill bit. Remove dust or wood shavings when done.

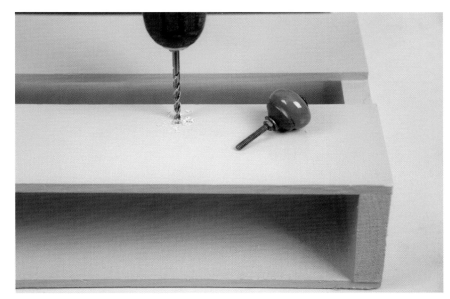

7 Insert knobs and attach, using pliers or a screwdriver if needed. Make sure the knobs are snug.

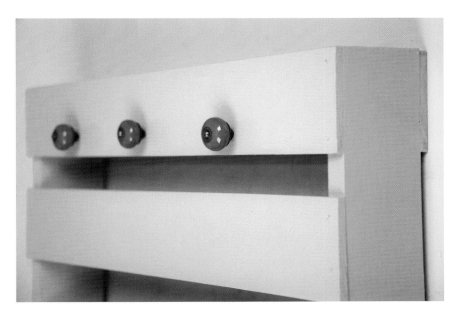

8 Hang the pallet on to a wall. Try to coordinate the sawtooth hangers with wall studs or use drywall screws for added support.

9 To paint a Mason jar, measure 3" up from the bottom and adhere a straight line with painter's tape.

10 Using a ¼" flat craft paintbrush, paint a Mason jar with white chalk paint. Chalk paint has great adhesion and can be used decoratively on glass.

11 Repeat steps 9 and 10 on the remaining two jars. Let dry. Apply a second coat of paint. Remove tape while paint is still wet. Let dry.

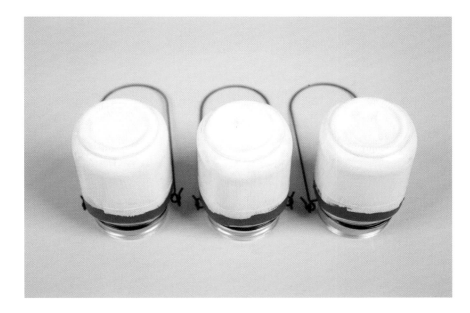

12 Hang the Mason jars on the cabinet hardware knobs. Fill the jars with your favorite flowers—fresh or faux!

TIP

A ³⁄₁₆" drill bit is the standard size for cabinet hardware, but be sure to check the decorative knobs to make sure you are using the correct size. Cabinet hardware can be found at local home improvement stores or craft stores.

PALLET WOOD DOMINOES

Backyard activities are favorite times together as a family. These oversize dominoes are a fun way to learn this traditional game. You will need enough pallet wood to make twenty-eight pieces. If you can't find enough pallets, try inexpensive fencing wood from a local hardware store. Not only is it the perfect width, it's already treated for outdoor use.

SUPPLIES YOU WILL NEED

- scrap pallet wood
- chop saw
- ruler
- pencil
- 100 grit sandpaper
- 220 grit sandpaper

- cotton cloth
- black outdoor craft paint
- small round craft paintbrush
- painter's tape
- 2" chip paintbrush
- waterproof varnish

1 Use these patterns as references for your pallet wood dominoes.

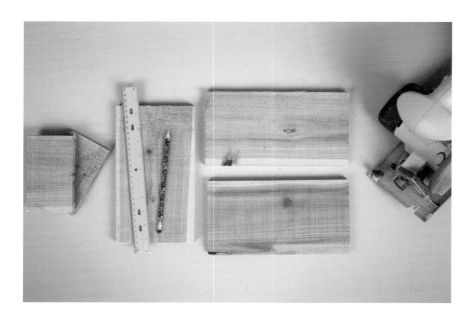

2 Prep the pallet wood by cutting twenty-eight pieces 4" x 8" with a chop saw. You can adjust the size according to the wood you have.

3 Smooth rough cut edges with 100 grit sandpaper. Use 220 grit sandpaper to smooth out entire surfaces and edges. Wipe away any dust with a clean dry cloth.

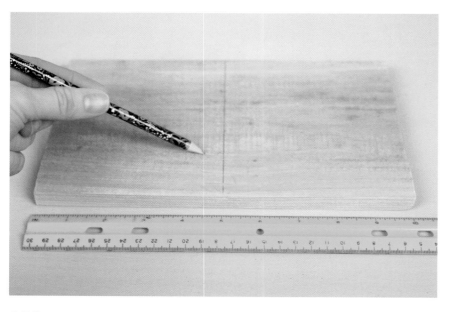

4 Lay the wood horizontally, one at a time, on a flat surface. Using a ruler and a pencil, measure and draw a straight line directly down the middle of each piece.

5 Using the provided domino patterns on page 99, measure and mark each dot placement. Draw a small *x* showing where each dot will be painted.

6 After marking all the wood, use black outdoor craft paint and a small round craft paintbrush to draw 1" circles by hand. Don't worry about the circles being perfect. The organic "rough" look is more fun.

7 Allow all the painted domino dots to dry. Using painter's tape, place a straight line of tape ¼" away from the drawn pencil line on either side, creating a ½" line. Press firmly on the tape for a good seal.

8 Using the same small craft paintbrush, paint the middle stripe on each piece of wood black.

9 Carefully remove the painter's tape while the paint is still wet.

10 Go back and touch up both the dots and stripes with black paint, as needed. Let dry completely.

11 Seal each domino on the front and back with waterproof varnish, using a 2" chip paintbrush. Let it completely dry and cure before use.

TIP

Wood dominoes can be used for more than just the traditional game. Use them like building blocks to create fun structures outdoors. When not in use, make (or buy) a crate for storage and keep them indoors to prevent additional wear and tear from the elements.

PALLET WOOD SIGN

Wooden crates don't have to be used just for storage. They are incredibly easy to disassemble for other fun home decor projects. The pallet pictured here was transformed into the perfect sign in just a few simple steps.

SUPPLIES YOU WILL NEED

- 12½" x 18" x 9½" wooden crate

- hammer

- needle-nose pliers

- 220 grit sandpaper

- cotton cloth

- wood glue

- two pieces of 1" x 1" x 12" craft balsa wood

- ½" nails

- acrylic paint in blue and off-white

- 2" chip paintbrush

- 10" wood letters HOME

- 1" chip paintbrush

- small round craft paintbrush

1 Deconstruct the wooden crate by removing the slats with a hammer. Carefully tap firmly on each slat from the inside, and it will gently pop right off.

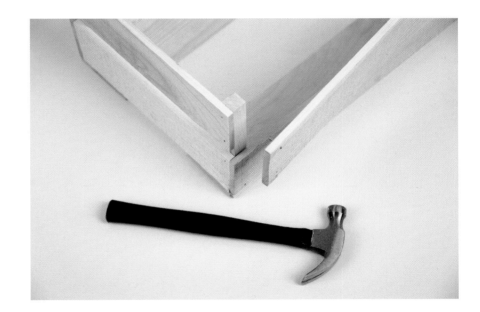

2 You will need six slats for this project, but you can remove some, depending on the desired size of the sign.

3 After taking apart the slats, remove any nails or staples with pliers. You may need to use a hammer to gently tap them out. Be careful not to split the wood.

4 Smooth any rough areas with sandpaper. When done, wipe away dust with a clean dry cloth.

5 Line up the slats vertically. Glue each balsa wood piece horizontally to the back of the sign, one on top and one on bottom. Let dry.

6 Reinforce the sign with nails on the back and front sides along the balsa wood. Use three to four nails on each piece.

7 Flip the sign facing upward and use blue paint and 2" paintbrush to paint the slats. Be sure the brush strokes follow the direction of the wood grain. Let dry.

8 Paint sign edges blue, flip over, and paint back side. Let dry. Add a second coat to entire sign, if needed.

9 Paint the top side and sides of the letters spelling HOME, using off-white paint and 1" paintbrush. Let dry. Paint a second coat, if needed.

10 Place letters in desired spot on sign and glue into place, using industrial-strength wood glue. Let dry.

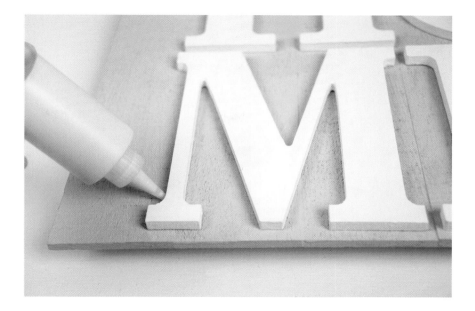

11 Using a small round craft paintbrush and off-white paint, hand-paint decorative leaf details along the sides of the letters. Let dry. Touch up, if needed.

TIP

Precut wood letters are available at major craft retailers, if you are not confident in your hand-lettering skills and can be a fun way to create custom seasonal signs and monograms.

PALLET WOOD STORAGE BOX

Simple boxes are a great introduction to woodworking, especially when using inexpensive reclaimed pallet wood. Try a variety of cutting tools to create the same results. With a little practice, your simple wood boxes will be functional decor in no time.

SUPPLIES YOU WILL NEED

- three scrap pallet wood pieces ¼" thick

- miter saw

- 220 grit sandpaper

- cotton cloth

- wood glue

- hammer

- ¾" nails

- 2" chip paintbrush

- chalk paint in light-gray and dark-brown

- paper towels

1 Cut the scrap pallet wood with a miter saw to equal three 3" x 14" pieces and two 3" x 3½" pieces. If the wood is thicker or thinner than ¼", adjust the measurements accordingly. If you are not able to find a wood pallet to deconstruct, use inexpensive pinewood or balsa wood from a local home improvement store.

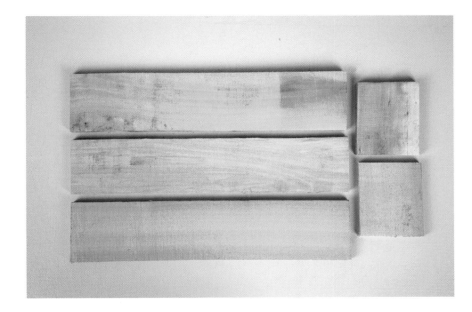

2 Smooth the cut edges and any other rough areas on the wood with sandpaper. Wipe away dust with a clean dry cloth.

3 Using industrial-strength wood glue, apply a straight line along one side of the long cut boards.

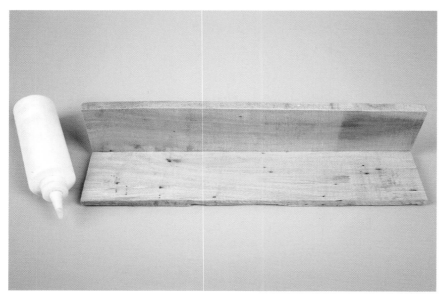

4 Adhere the wood box base and one side together. Hold in place for a few minutes while it sets.

5 Repeat on the other side, applying a straight thin line of glue. Position the second side in place, holding it for a few minutes while it sets. Allow it to dry completely.

6 Adhere the two end pieces in place with wood glue. Let them dry completely. Use heavy-duty wood clamps to hold in place, if needed.

7 Gently hammer nails into sides and bottom of box for extra reinforcement and avoid splitting the wood. Your nail length will depend on the thickness of the wood. For a ¼" board, ¾" to 1" nails are ideal.

8 Use a dry-brush technique to paint the box. Dip a paintbrush into the light-gray chalk paint and gently wipe off most of the paint on to a paper towel.

9 Holding the paintbrush to the wood, gently go back and forth using long strokes, following the wood grain. Let the paintbrush lightly touch the surface, creating thin contrasting lines. This technique will give the wood a distressed look by creating visual depth and contrast.

10 Continue dry brushing the insides of the box with light-gray paint. Let dry completely.

11 For added visual texture, dry brush dark-brown chalk paint on the outside and inside of the box. Let dry completely.

TIP

Instead of using sandpaper to distress painted projects, dry brushing is a good way to create visual texture without the mess. Try painting your project a solid color first and then dry brush a light and dark shade on top. Play around with different colors for a unique look.

DECOUPAGE CRATE

Patterned paper is an easy way to decorate a wooden crate without having to spend a lot of time painting. Not only can decoupage make it look professionally painted, its natural glue formula also acts as a protective sealant. Most papers, whether thick or thin, will work with decoupage glue. When you get tired of a design, just decoupage a new pattern paper on top!

SUPPLIES YOU WILL NEED

- 12½" x 18" x 9½" wooden crate
- 220 grit sandpaper
- cotton cloth
- white chalk paint
- 2" chip paintbrush
- ruler

- pencil
- scissors
- 1" chip paintbrush
- decoupage glue
- decorative paper
- decorative corner brackets (optional)

1 Prep the crate by sanding any uneven surfaces or rough areas. Make sure the exterior slats have a smooth finish. Wipe away dust with a clean dry cloth.

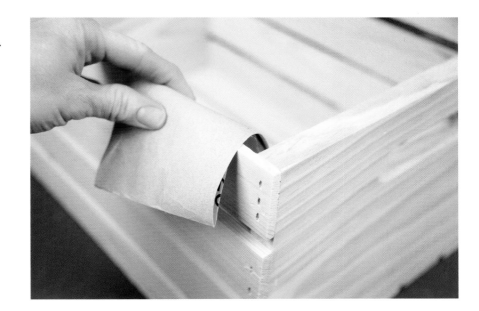

2 Paint the crate with white chalk paint, using a 2" chip paintbrush. Work from the inside out and be sure to paint in between the slats. Let dry.

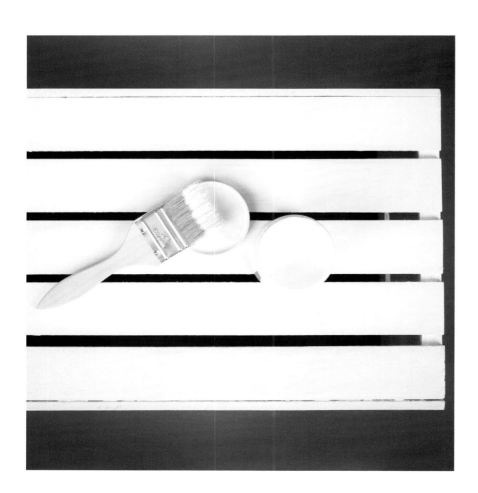

3 Apply a second coat of white chalk paint. You should have a smooth matte finish when done. Let dry completely.

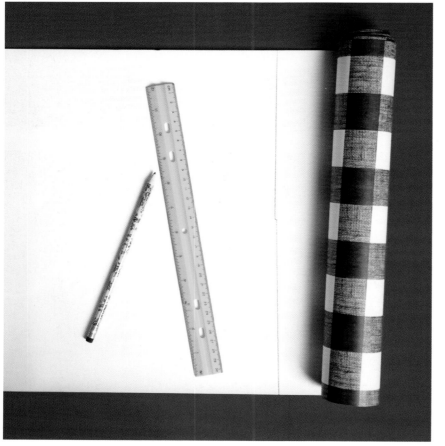

4 Measure the crate ends and slats before trimming the decorative paper. You will need two end pieces for the front and back handle sides and eight long pieces for the slats. Measure ⅛" on the inside of each section being covered, so you have a little white edge showing around each decoupage piece of paper. For a 12½" x 18" x 9½" crate, the front and back pieces should measure 9" x 12" and the slat paper should measure 2" x 12".

5 Cut the paper to size according to your measurements. For larger paper rolls, you can use a rotary cutter and a ruler instead of scissors.

6 After cutting the paper for the front and back, use a pencil to trace the two handle openings and cut out.

7 For the side slats, make sure the paper pattern matches up when placed next to each other. You can check this by laying out the strips in the desired order.

8 To decoupage the crate, use a 1" chip paintbrush to adhere a thin coat of decoupage glue to the painted wood area you wish to cover. Add a second thin coat of glue to the paper underside.

9 Carefully lay the paper in place, smoothing out any wrinkles with your hands. Apply a thin coat of decoupage glue on top. Smooth out additional wrinkles. Let dry. Depending on the type of paper, add a second coat of glue on top if needed.

10 Attach decorative corner brackets to the crate's top four corners. These brass elements are available at home improvement stores and often come with nails required for installation.

11 Display the crate in a visible spot and fill it up with your favorite decor items.

TIP

Thicker decorative paper tends to warp more with moisture and benefits from being lightly misted with water before applying decoupage glue. Thinner paper, like tissue paper, can be applied with a single coat of glue but needs to be handled carefully. Craft manufacturers make lovely waxlike decorative paper intended specifically for decoupage and is by far the easiest to apply. The paper is prestretched and handles moisture very well.

ROLLER TOY BOX

Cleaning up toys can be tedious. This cute crate can easily be pulled along, making it easy for little ones to help! It also makes for a convenient way for kids to move favorite toys from room to room.

SUPPLIES YOU WILL NEED

- 12½" x 18" x 9½" wooden crate
- 220 grit sandpaper
- cotton cloth
- 2" paintbrush
- red satin acrylic paint
- drill

- ⅛" drill bit
- four swivel plate casters
- screwdriver
- ¼" screws
- decorative knob
- muslin fabric
- scissors

- straight pins
- pencil
- black fabric craft paint
- small round craft paintbrush
- fabric glue
- twine

1 Prep the crate by lightly going over any rough areas with sandpaper. Wipe away dust with a clean dry cloth.

2 Paint the crate, working from the inside out, with red satin acrylic paint. Let dry.

3 Paint a second coat and let dry. Red paint often needs multiple coats, so apply a third coat as needed. The raw wood is very absorbent, so make sure you are seeing a nice satin finish for durability. If the sheen feels flat, add an additional coat of paint. Let dry completely.

4 Prep the crate for the casters with a drill and drill bit. Go slowly and be careful, so you don't split the delicate wood.

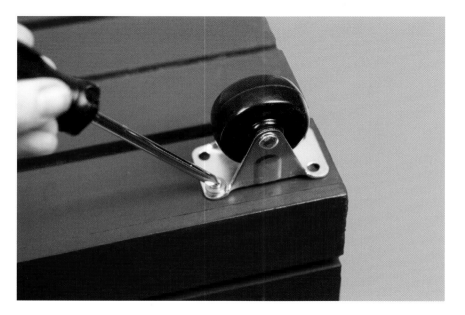

5 Attach the four casters, using screws.

6 On the front of the painted crate, use the drill and drill bit to make a hole for a decorative knob. You may need to adjust the size of the drill bit according to the hardware you use. Wipe away any dust or wood shavings.

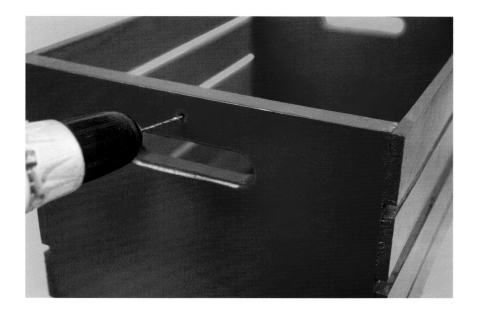

7 Attach a decorative knob to the crate. If by chance the hardware is too long, trim the excess with bolt cutters.

8 To make a sign for the crate, get a printed pattern and additional supplies together. These include straight pins, a pencil, black fabric craft paint, a craft paintbrush, and scissors.

9 Use straight pins to hold printed template and fabric together. Cut pennant shape out of fabric with scissors and remove pins when finished.

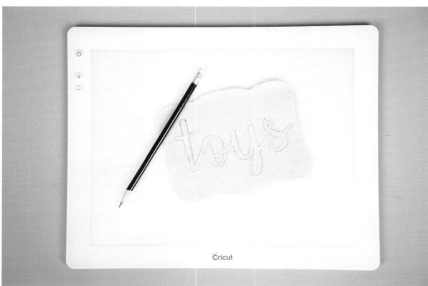

10 Use a light table or window to transfer the lettering to the fabric with a pencil.

11 Paint lettering with black fabric craft paint, using a small round paintbrush. Let dry. Add a second coat, if needed.

12 Use fabric glue or a hot glue gun to attach twine to back of sign for hanging. Let dry completely.

13 Hang the sign on the decorative knob and fill the crate with the children's favorite toys.

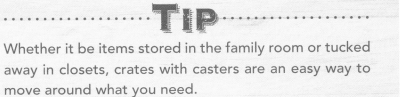

TIP

Whether it be items stored in the family room or tucked away in closets, crates with casters are an easy way to move around what you need.

CRATE DOLL WARDROBE

My youngest daughter has become quite the doll collector. Not only does her favorite doll have a special place to sleep at night, it has quite an array of clothing too! It made sense for the doll to have its own itty-bitty closet to store them in. A wooden crate makes an ideal storage space and can be transformed into a doll wardrobe in just a few easy steps!

SUPPLIES YOU WILL NEED

- pinewood measuring at least 9" x 12"
- measuring tape
- pencil
- chop saw
- 9" wood dowel
- 220 grit sandpaper
- cotton cloth
- 2" chip paintbrush
- acrylic craft paint in red, blue, and white
- 12½" x 18" x 9½" wooden crate
- four craft wood candlestick holders
- 1" chip paintbrush
- screwdriver
- ½" screws
- four 1" zinc-plated corner braces
- ¼" screws
- wood glue
- decorative corner brackets (optional)

1 Measure and cut pinewood or scrap wood to 9" x 12", using a chop saw. Cut wood dowel down to 9". Using sandpaper, smooth cuts and any other rough areas. Wipe away dust with a clean dry cloth.

2 Using the 2" chip paintbrush and red paint, paint the dowel on the front and back sides. Let dry. Paint a second coat, if needed.

3 Paint the 9" x 12" wood piece with the same red paint. Let dry. Apply a second coat, if needed. This will be the storage shelf, so you will want to paint all sides.

4 While the dowel and shelf dry, sand any rough areas on the crate. Wipe away dust with a clean dry cloth.

5 Paint the entire crate, inside and outside, with blue paint. Use long brush strokes, following the grain of the wood. Let dry. Paint a second coat, if needed.

6 Paint the craft wood candlestick tops and sides with white paint and 1" chip paintbrush. You do not need to paint the bottoms. Let dry.

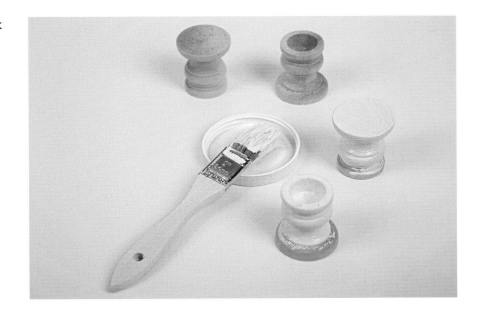

7 Check the shelf and dowel to make sure they fit snuggly inside the crate. Add additional coats of paint, if needed.

8 To attach the dowel, turn the crate vertically right side up. On the second slat from the back, measure 3" down from the top. Holding the dowel in place, insert a ½" screw into the crate and dowel. Do not tighten all the way. Repeat on the left side and then tighten both screws.

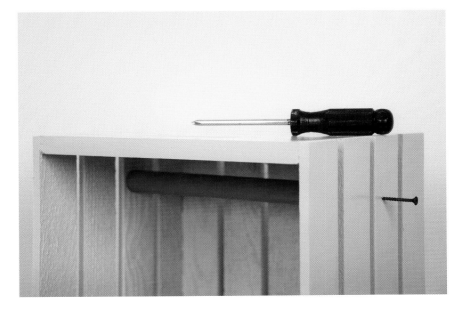

9 Paint the screw exteriors with blue paint.

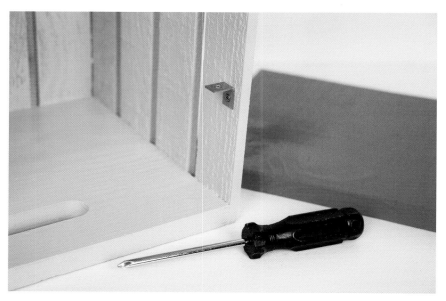

10 To attach the shelf, get the four 1" corner braces and ¼" screws. Measuring 4" from the base of the crate, attach two braces near the front and two braces in the back.

11 Carefully slide the shelf into place. Use four additional ¼" screws to attach the shelf from the bottom, or leave the shelf as is so it can be removed easily.

12 Turn the crate upside down and attach the four candlestick holders using industrial-strength wood glue. Place one leg in each of the four corners of the crate. Let dry.

13 Turn the crate right side up and adhere decorative corner brackets, if desired. Fill the crate doll wardrobe with plastic hangers, clothes, and accessories!

For a storage closet that opens and closes, attach two wooden crate pieces with hinges and magnetic closure hardware.

CRATE TOOLBOX

There is no reason your tools and supplies can't be kept in something functional and pretty. A handmade caddy is a superb way to customize storage and makes transporting tools around a breeze!

SUPPLIES YOU WILL NEED

- ¾" whitewood board
- ruler
- pencil
- jigsaw
- 220 grit sandpaper
- cotton cloth
- 2½" balsa wood slats
- hammer
- ½" nails
- wood filler
- yellow craft paint
- 2" chip paintbrush
- tree branch
- 1" nails

1 Use a ruler and a pencil on whitewood board to measure two rectangles at 5¼" x 9½".

2 At the top center of the rectangle, measure and draw a line in the middle one inch wide. From the bottom of the rectangle, measure and mark six inches on each side. Draw a line connecting the markings, creating a house shape.

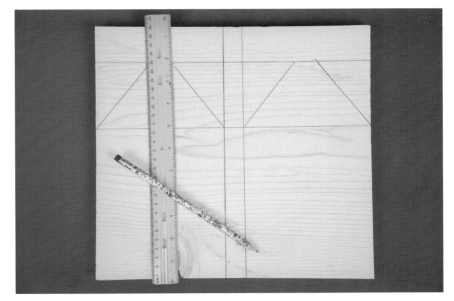

3 Using a jigsaw, cut the house shape along the lines.

4 Smooth the cut lines with sandpaper. Wipe away dust with a clean dry cloth.

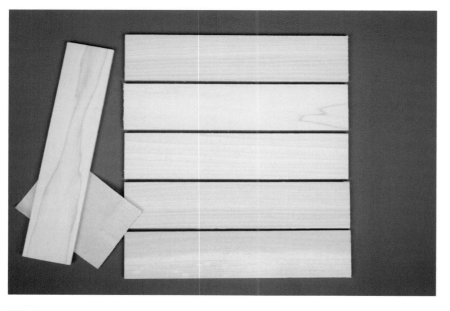

5 Cut the balsa wood slats down to 10" long. You will need a total of six pieces. Sand the cut lines and wipe away dust with a clean dry cloth.

6 To assemble the toolbox, set the front wood piece upright, holding the bottom right-hand wood slat in place. Gently hammer ½" nails to secure it in place. Attach the back piece in the same manner. Once you have a slat attached to the right side, attach the bottom slat on the left side.

7 Use additional ½" nails to attach the upper side slats and bottom slats. Use one to two nails per slat on each side. Fill nail holes with wood filler, if desired.

8 Paint the toolbox in yellow craft paint. Let dry. Paint a second coat, if needed.

9 Make sure the tree branch is fully dry on the inside. It also should feel dry and brittle on the outside. Remove any twigs or rough areas. Cut the branch to 8½" long and sand the cut area.

10 Attach the handle to the finished toolbox, using a hammer and 1" nails. Secure the branch in place with nails in two different areas on each side, so the handle is firmly in place.

11 Fill the toolbox with your favorite tools or creative essentials!

TIP

After assembly, the toolbox will measure 11½" long. To shorten or lengthen it, make adjustments to the balsa wood length, keeping the pieces the same size.

CRATE PET CADDY

Pet food bowls and containers can be bulky and eyesores. They are also easy to tip over and spill. Help establish a consistent routine and an attractive eating spot for your pet by creating a cozy food station for fresh food and water!

SUPPLIES YOU WILL NEED

- 12½" x 18" x 9½" wooden crate
- two 6" metal bowls
- pen or pencil
- jigsaw
- 100 grit sandpaper
- 220 grit sandpaper

- cotton cloth
- wood glue (optional)
- 2" chip paintbrush
- acrylic paint in charcoal-black, light-gray, and off-white
- paper towels
- water-based semigloss varnish

1 Turn the crate upside down. Center two metal bowls in the middle, leaving about ½" in between them.

2 Using a pen or pencil, draw a line around each bowl, creating cut lines.

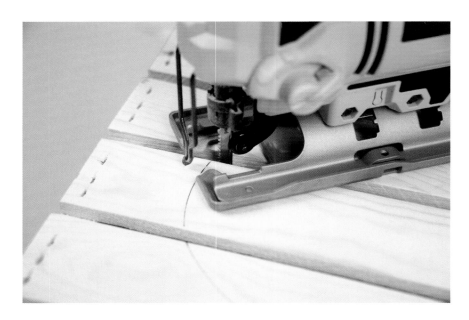

3 With a jigsaw, cut ¼" inside the drawn lines. Be certain not to cut outside the lines or your bowls will not fit properly.

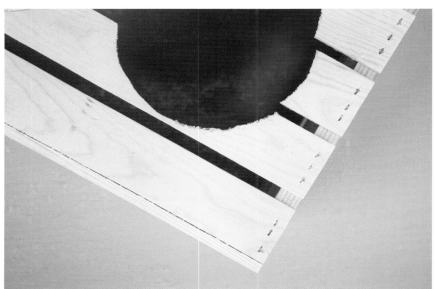

4 Carefully remove the inner wood circles and use 100 grit sandpaper to smooth out rough edges. Sand away pencil lines.

5 Go over the cut lines again with 220 grit sandpaper. Since this pet caddy is for your favorite furry friend, be sure to sand and smooth out all rough areas. Wipe away dust with a clean dry cloth.

6 Depending on the crate, you may need to use wood glue to reattach the center slat. When dry, paint the entire crate, inside and outside, with charcoal-black paint. Let dry. Add a second coat, if needed.

7 When the paint is dry, dry-brush light-gray paint by dipping the paintbrush in the paint and then wiping most of it off on to a paper towel. Lightly brush back and forth in long strokes along the wood grain. Dry-brush crate sides, rotating the crate as you go.

8 Repeat dry-painting on the top of the crate in long strokes, following the wood grain. Let dry completely before moving on to the next step.

9 Using off-white paint, repeat dry-painting by dipping the paintbrush in paint first and then wiping most of it off on to a paper towel. Dry-brush each side of the crate, rotating as you go.

10 Use the same light brisk motions to apply off-white paint to your crate top, working in between each slat. Let dry completely.

11 When the paint is dry, apply a generous coat of water-based semigloss varnish. This will help protect the crate from any food or moisture. Allow the crate at least two to three days to fully dry and cure before use.

12 When dry, place the metal bowls inside the caddy and fill them up with treats for your pet!

TIP

For smaller pets, cut the crate height in half by removing two slats on the bottom of each side and using a jigsaw to cut the wood supports in half.

Crate Puppet Theater

You are never too old to put on a puppet show! Use your favorite toys and stuffed animals to entertain children with this whimsical theater. The wooden crates provide excellent storage between shows, and you can easily customize the sign for your latest production.

SUPPLIES YOU WILL NEED

- two 12½" x 18" x 9½" wooden crates
- 220 grit sandpaper
- cotton cloth
- 2" chip paintbrush
- acrylic paint in blue and silver
- two 1" metal mending plates
- ¼" screws
- screwdriver
- 2" x 2" x 24" wood
- pencil
- measuring tape
- miter saw
- two 12" table legs
- 6½" x 12" wood sign
- 1" chip paintbrush
- black chalkboard paint
- ½" wood measuring 7" x 26½"
- wood glue
- drill
- ¼" drill bit
- two 2½" furring strips measuring 32"
- 1" screws
- ¾" screws
- wood clothespin
- twine
- two 9" wood dowels
- two fat quarters of fabric
- craft glue
- decorative molding

1 Smooth crates thoroughly with sandpaper, removing any rough areas. Wipe away dust with a clean dry cloth. With a 2" chip paintbrush, paint both crates with blue acrylic paint, working from the inside out. Let dry.

2 Apply a second coat of blue paint, covering both front and back. Let dry.

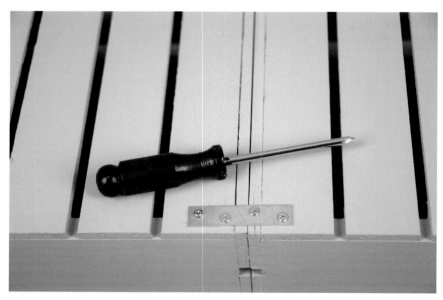

3 Lay the crates facedown, side-by-side, vertically. Attach crates with mending plates and ¼" screws.

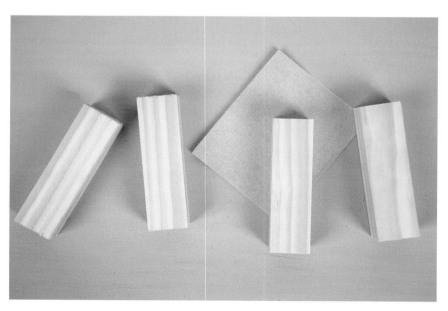

4 Create wood legs by cutting 2" x 2" x 24" wood into four 6" pieces, using a miter saw. Smooth cut edges with sandpaper. Wipe away dust with a clean dry cloth.

5 Using 2" chip paintbrush, paint four pieces of wood with silver acrylic paint. Let dry. Paint second coat, if needed.

6 Paint the two table legs with the same silver acrylic paint. Let dry.

7 Paint the wood sign with 1" chip brush and black chalkboard paint. Paint front and back in *horizontal* brushstrokes. Let dry. Paint a second coat on both sides in *vertical* brushstrokes. Let dry.

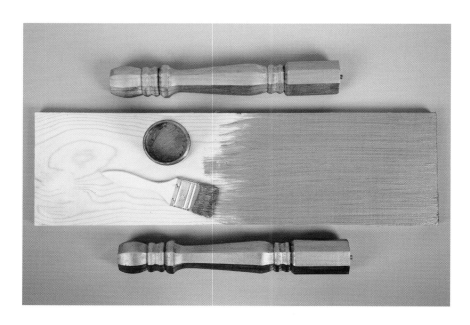

8 Add a second coat of silver paint to the table legs and paint the 7" x 26½" wood with the same color. Let dry.

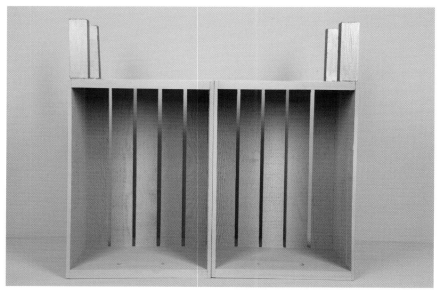

9 Turn the crates upside down and attach the four painted pieces of wood with industrial-strength wood glue. Let dry.

10 Turn the theater right side up. Using a drill and drill bit, make a hole on the front left-hand corner and a hole on the front right-hand corner of the attached crates. Remove any dust or shavings.

11 Screw the two table legs into place on the left-hand and right-hand sides of the attached crates.

12 Paint the two furring strips silver on the front, back, and sides. Let dry.

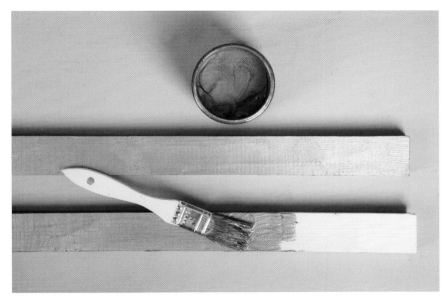

13 Attach furring strips to each side of the attached crates, using a 1" screw at the top and one at the bottom. Attach 7" x 26½" wood to the top of the furring strips, using a drill and ¾" screws.

14 Adhere wood clothespin to attached crates' front center, using wood glue. Hang sign. Use chalk or chalk pen to embellish sign. Using wood glue, attach dowels to top front of crates and adhere gathered fabric to dowels with craft glue. Add additional decorative molding as desired.

TIP

To condition the chalkboard, rub a plain piece of chalk all over the surface and wipe it off with a clean dry paper towel in a circular motion. This will allow chalk particles to fill the paint. You will find writing and erasing much better after performing this technique!

ABOUT THE AUTHOR

Natalie Wright works full time as a creative director for an overseas home decor manufacturer. She travels often for her job but is happiest crafting and creating at home in Lexington, Kentucky, with her family, which includes her husband, their four children, and a puppy named Pulgi. Natalie is the author of other Dover Publications titles, *Slime 101: How to Make Stretchy, Fluffy, Glittery & Colorful Slime!* and *Modern Frames and Garlands* in the popular series Make in a Day, and writes a blog called Natalme about paper crafting, parties, and mixed-media projects.